# WILDLIFE AT RISK

# PANDAS

Gillian Standring

The Bookwright Press
New York · 1991

# WILDLIFE AT RISK

Bears
Birds of Prey
Elephants
Gorillas
Monkeys
Pandas
Rhinos
Seals
Tigers
Whales and Dolphins

**Cover:** A giant panda eating its favorite food, fresh bamboo.

DP

First published in the
United States in 1991 by
The Bookwright Press
387 Park Avenue South
New York, NY 10016

First published in 1991 by
Wayland (Publishers) Ltd
61 Western Road, Hove,
East Sussex  BN3 1JD, England

**Library of Congress
Cataloging-in-Publication Data**

Standring, Gillian.
    Pandas / Gillian Standring.
      p. cm. – (Wildlife at risk)
    Includes bibliographical references and index.
    Summary: Looks at the physical characteristics, behavior, and life cycle of the panda in the wild and in captivity, and focuses on efforts to save this endangered species from extinction.
    ISBN 0–531–18397–1
    1. Giant panda – Juvenile literature. 2. Endangered species – Juvenile literature. 3. Wildlife conservation – Juvenile literature. [1. Giant panda. 2. Pandas. 3. Rare animals. 4. Wildlife conservation.] I. Title. II. Series.
QL737.C214S73 1991
599.74'443–dc20                      90–21969
                                              CIP
                                              AC

Typeset by Kalligraphic Design Ltd
Printed in Italy by L.E.G.O. S.p.A.

# Contents

All words printed in **bold** are explained
in the glossary on page 30.

# INTRODUCING PANDAS

The giant panda is one of the best-known animals in the world. It is also one of the rarest. In 1990 there were only about one thousand giant pandas living wild in China, and only fifteen in zoos outside China. So if you have seen pandas in a zoo you are very lucky.

Pandas have lived in China for thousands of years but there have never been many of them. They were highly valued by the ancient Chinese emperors. Few travelers from Europe visited China until the late nineteenth century. In 1869 a French priest, Father Armand David,

*Giant pandas live in the mountains of southwest China. Winters can be very cold here.*

discovered the fabulous "black and white bear" and brought its skin and bones back from China to be studied by scientists in Paris. The first living pandas outside China were brought to the United States in 1936 and to Britain in 1938.

## Giant Panda

Scientific name: *Ailuropoda melanoleuca*

Chinese names: Bei-shung (white bear) Da-shiungmao (big bear cat)

Height at shoulder: 31 in (male) (on all fours)          28 in (female)

Height standing: max. 5ft 6in

Weight:   330 lb (male) 265 lb (female)

Life span:  12 years (in wild)

Gestation period: 125 – 150 days

Distribution: Mountain bamboo forests of southwest China

These are the Chinese characters for Giant Panda.

big

bear

cat

Ever since, the giant panda has been of great interest to scientists, zoo-keepers and all animal lovers. Because it is so popular and so unusual, it was chosen as the symbol of the World Wildlife Fund (WWF), the world's best-known **conservation** organization.

One of the mysteries about pandas is who their animal relatives are. We can quite easily see that cats belong to the same large family as lions and tigers, and that wolves are similar to our pet dogs. But there are no other animals very like pandas.

The lesser, or red, panda was discovered in 1825. It may be the closest relative to

*A raccoon's face mask and striped tail make it look a bit like a red panda.*

*Like giant pandas, red pandas eat bamboo.*

the giant black and white panda, although they don't look much alike. They both come from the same part of the world, eat similar food and both have special front paws, which they use to hold their food. But red pandas are more like raccoons, so perhaps giant pandas are also related to raccoons.

*Giant pandas look similar to bears and walk with a flat-footed waddle, just like a bear.*

Giant pandas are often wrongly called "panda bears" or "bamboo bears." They certainly look like bears. Their size and shape, and their fur, teeth and claws all remind us of a bear. Pandas walk and climb just like bears, too. Some scientists now think that giant pandas really are more like bears than like red pandas. Other people think that the giant panda is **unique** and should be given a special place all to itself in the **zoology** books. We shall probably never solve this panda riddle.

# LIFE IN THE WILD

Pandas, unlike people, prefer to be cool and damp. Hot, dry weather is bad for them. High up in the mountains of Sichuan in southwest China, there are thick, misty forests where it is always cool and damp. Pandas spend most of the year in these forests. In winter they come down to the lower slopes to get away from the deep snow and freezing cold. There are few people living in this part of China.

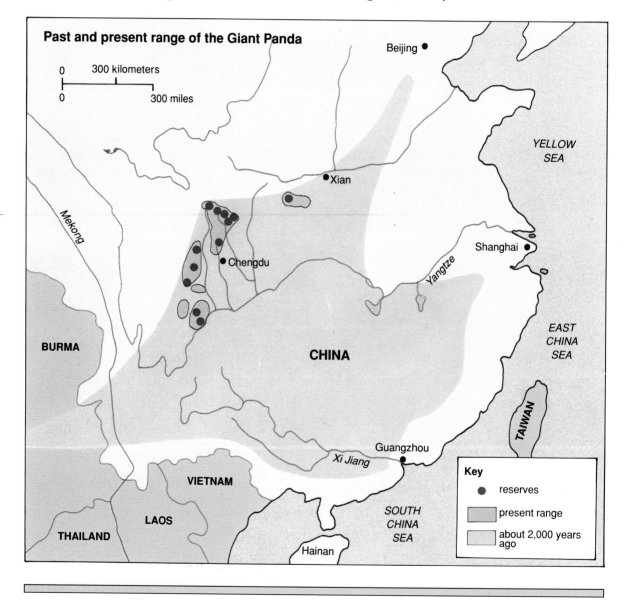

Past and present range of the Giant Panda

0    300 kilometers

0    300 miles

Beijing ●

Xian ●

YELLOW SEA

Mekong

Chengdu ●

Shanghai ●

Yangtze

BURMA

CHINA

EAST CHINA SEA

TAIWAN

Xi Jiang

Guangzhou ●

VIETNAM

LAOS

THAILAND

SOUTH CHINA SEA

Hainan

Key

● reserves

present range

about 2,000 years ago

The forests where the pandas live are mainly dense thickets of bamboos growing more than 10 feet (3 m) high. Bamboos have hard, tough stems and narrow, pointed leaves like giant grasses. All kinds of other plants grow in the bamboo forest too, including many now grown in European gardens.

*The golden takin is an unusual antelope that lives in the same area as pandas.*

*Beautiful rhododendrons grow in the mountain forests where pandas live.*

The bamboo forests are also the home of **rare** golden monkeys, takin antelopes, leopards, wild dogs, bears and porcupines. None of these animals are much danger to a grown panda. It can climb trees to reach safety or defend itself with its strong teeth and claws.

Pandas are famous for eating bamboo. Their food grows all around them in the bamboo forests, so they never have to hunt for it. However, they like to eat only a few kinds of bamboo, and their **digestion** is not very good, so they spend almost all the day just eating. Pandas also eat grasses, roots, bulbs and tree bark. Sometimes they catch little cane rats and fish. They often take long drinks from mountain streams and rivers.

*A panda rests by a cool mountain waterfall with some fresh bamboo close at hand.*

The panda's favorite bamboo, sometimes called chinacane, is a bit like sugarcane. Pandas eat the leaves and young shoots, but the best part is the sweet, juicy pith inside the stems. A panda has a special way of feeding, sitting upright with its back propped against a tree.

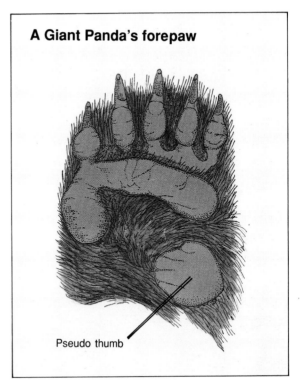

**A Giant Panda's forepaw**

Pseudo thumb

*A panda uses its forepaws to hold bamboo while feeding.*

It bites off a length of bamboo and uses its forepaws to hold the food to its mouth. First a panda strips off the tough outer part of the cane, then it crushes the pith with its large, strong jaws and teeth.

The giant panda and red panda each have a unique kind of thumb on each forepaw, which helps them to grip the bamboo. The "thumb" is a special enlarged wrist bone covered by a leathery pad.

A panda's life is very lazy and peaceful. A wild panda is surrounded by its food and has few enemies, so by day it just moves leisurely around, feeding as it goes. At night it sleeps, usually in a cave among rocks or under a fallen tree stump. In zoos, pandas sleep for much of the day between their meals.

Although pandas walk clumsily with a flat-footed waddle while on the ground, they are agile climbers and sometimes sleep up in trees. Young pandas are playful and acrobatic, even hanging upside-down from branches. They also enjoy splashing in water, although they don't often swim.

*Pandas in zoos take long naps between meals. This one is in the Toronto Zoo, Canada.*

Pandas like to live alone. A full-grown panda can look after itself and does not often meet other pandas, since they are spread out among the mountain bamboo forests. If two pandas meet, they will leave each other alone and

*In the wild, pandas often climb trees for safety.*

go their separate ways, unless it is the **breeding season**. As they are **solitary** animals, wild pandas are very hard to find and to study.

# PANDAS AND THEIR YOUNG

Pandas can begin to have young when they are about 6 years old. Male and female pandas look exactly alike, even to each other. During the short breeding season every spring (usually in April), a female panda who is ready to **mate** leaves scent messages for the male. She does this by rubbing her bottom on rocks and plants, and also makes quite loud bleating noises. Male pandas living nearby smell and hear her signals and can find her easily. After the female has mated with one male, she drives other males away.

*Male and female pandas rarely meet in the wild.*

Five months later, usually in September, one or two panda **cubs** are born. The mother looks after her young alone. A new-born panda is the size of a rat and weighs about 3 to 4 ounces (100 g). It is pink with thin white fur and is totally helpless. About a month later the cub has the special black and white panda pattern.

A panda cub starts to crawl at about 3 months old, when it weighs over 6 pounds (2.7 kg). It is big enough to look after itself at about 6 months old. When it is 4 years old, it will be full grown and weigh about 220 pounds (100 kg).

*Left A panda cub explores its surroundings in Sichuan, China.*

*Below A day-old panda looks like a small white rat.*

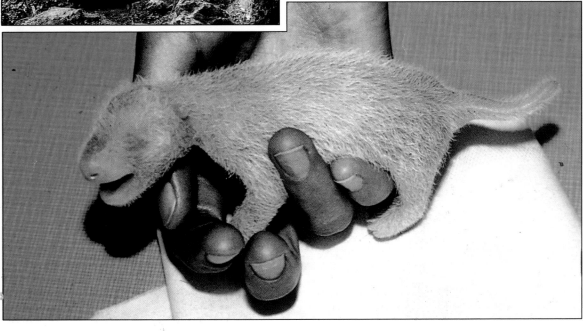

# WHY ARE PANDAS SO RARE?

## Disappearing bamboo

Giant pandas have probably never been common anywhere. There are several reasons for this. They do not produce many babies. As we have seen, they can live only in cool bamboo forests. Each panda needs a big area of forest to itself, and even large areas of suitable mountain forest have room for only a few pandas.

*These are the mountain forests of Sichuan where pandas live. In such dense forests, pandas rarely meet.*

Pandas also need plenty of their favorite bamboo. This plant has a very unusual way of growing. For perhaps a hundred years, bamboo plants spread by underground branches. Then suddenly, all the bamboo plants over a wide area flower, make seeds and die. This leaves no food for the pandas until new plants grow from the seeds. Many pandas die of **starvation** when this happens, as it did in 1975–6.

*A bamboo grove provides plenty of food for a hungry panda.*

*The forests of Sichuan are being cut down to make room for villages and provide land for crops.*

For thousands of years, the giant panda's homeland in southwest China was very hard for people to reach, so it was left undisturbed for pandas and other wildlife. Now the millions of Chinese people need more land for their farms and villages. Modern roads help them to reach even the farthest mountains of Sichuan. As the people cut down the mountain forests, the pandas have fewer unspoiled bamboo groves to live in.

# The panda trade

Another reason why pandas are rare is that people have captured them from the wild. Since pandas were first brought out of China, zoos around the world have wanted to have their own pandas to attract crowds of visitors. In the past, expensive **expeditions** were sent to China to catch and bring back wild pandas. Fortunately

*Pandas are always popular in zoos. Here Chia-Chia at the London Zoo is visited by three Chinese children.*

those days are now over. The People's Republic of China banned the hunting of pandas in 1962. Now zoos can only obtain pandas as a gift from the Chinese people or from other zoos.

However, panda-hunting still goes on in spite of the ban. The pandas are not captured to be taken to zoos but are killed for their skins. Panda fur is too coarse to use for fur coats, but some people like to have a panda skin to decorate their home. In Japan people will pay a great deal (over $200,000) to have a black and white panda skin rug on the floor.

Of course, this hunting is against the law and if the hunters are caught they are imprisoned for life, or even sentenced to death. However, the hunters still manage to smuggle a few panda skins out of China. They take the risk because they are well paid by the people who want the panda skins.

*The giant panda's fur is too coarse to make coats but is sometimes used to make rugs.*

# SAVING THE PANDA

## Panda reserves

Although pandas are in danger from hunting, the main threat to them is the loss of their bamboo forests. There is some good news for pandas, however. The Chinese people and international conservation organizations are working hard to protect them.

Now there are twelve special panda **reserves** in China, where some 450 pandas are living in safety.

**Above** *There is plenty of bamboo growing in the panda reserves.*

**Left** *These Chinese workers are moving a panda to an area within a reserve, where it can live in safety.*

*The Wolong Research and Conservation Center. You can see cages where pandas are kept while scientists study them.*

The reserves were created to protect the pandas and the bamboo forests they need. The cutting down of bamboo and felling of trees by people is strictly controlled. Armed guards patrol the reserves to protect the pandas from hunters and to ensure that local people do not destroy the trees.

Besides protecting the pandas, it is important to tell the local people why these animals are so special. So the people from 5,000 villages in Sichuan are taught about the need to protect pandas and how to care for starving pandas. They are told why they should not cut down trees and bamboo. If a panda causes damage to the local people's farm crops, the people are paid to cover the damage.

The largest reserve, at Wolong, was created in 1975. In 1980 the Chinese government and WWF built a special panda-breeding and research center there.

# Breeding pandas

Every big zoo still wants to have giant pandas. Of course, one reason for this is that pandas always attract crowds of visitors. But another reason is that zoos around the world are trying to save pandas from becoming **extinct**. Zoos can offer pandas a safe home while helping them to **breed.**

Pandas kept in zoos need comfortable enclosures with an area of grass to lie on and some hard ground to wear down their claws. Tree trunks to lean against and climb on, and a pool to bathe in are also important. Pandas also like a private den and rocks and logs on which to leave their scent messages.

*A zoo-keeper with a panda cub in the Beijing Zoo, China. Notice the rocks and climbing frame for the panda to use.*

In the summer pandas must have plenty of cool shade.

A special diet for giant pandas **in captivity** keeps them healthy for twenty years or more. The pandas are usually given some fresh bamboo, along with other food that is easier to buy locally. Most zoos now have full-time **vets**, and some even have special hospitals to look after sick animals. So all zoo pandas are well cared for.

*Zoo pandas need plenty of bamboo to keep healthy. These pandas live in the Guangzhou Zoo, China.*

## Menu for a panda

| | |
|---|---|
| Boiled rice | 4.5 lb |
| Monkey pellets (for bran, bone meal and minerals) | 2 lb |
| Boiled eggs | 4 |
| Milk | 2 quarts |
| Honey | 1 tablespoon |
| Vitamin tablets | 4 |
| Minced meat | (every other day) |
| Fresh bamboo | 14 lb |

This is the daily food eaten by a panda at the London Zoo.

If zoos want to keep pandas, they must help each other to breed them. Zoos can lend each other pandas for breeding. In the 1960s, a panda from the London Zoo (Chi-Chi) and one from the Moscow Zoo (An-An) were brought together in the hope that they would mate.

*Chia-Chia getting to know the female panda, Ching-Ching.*

But nothing came of it. Since 1988, Chia-Chia, the London Zoo's male panda, has been in the Mexico City Zoo, where there are young female pandas. He has now mated with more than one of them.

On the way to Mexico, he stopped off at the Cincinnati Zoo, in Ohio, to raise money to help other pandas, too.

Zoos around the world have studied and examined their pandas to try to help them breed. As a result, vets and scientists now know much more about what goes on inside a panda. All this knowledge is shared by other zoos. The panda **stud-book**, kept at the London Zoo, records the important details of all zoo pandas. It helps zoos to plan their future breeding attempts.

*A vet examines Ching-Ching in the animal hospital at London Zoo.*

Instead of sending pandas on expensive worldwide breeding visits, scientists have now found a simpler, cheaper way. They collect **sperm** from a full-grown male panda and freeze it in a little tube to keep it fresh. Then they can send the tube from one zoo to another, and put the sperm into a female panda who is ready to mate. This method is called **artificial insemination**. It was tried successfully with the female panda Shao-Shao at the Madrid Zoo. In 1982 she had a baby from Chia-Chia after her own mate had died. Baby pandas have also been born in other zoos as a result of artificial insemination.

*In September 1963, Ming-Ming was the first panda cub successfully reared in captivity. Here it plays with its mother, Li-Li.*

*A mother panda holds her month-old cub, which was born in the breeding center at Wolong in China.*

Panda cubs born in zoos often die very young. No one has yet managed to bring up a bottle-fed baby panda when its mother could not look after it. There is still a lot to find out about caring for mother pandas and their cubs.

At the panda-breeding center in the Chinese Wolong reserve, international experts are studying the panda's breeding habits. So far, only one cub has been born there, but scientists hope to breed more in the future.

# THE FUTURE FOR PANDAS

The giant panda is a strange and wonderful animal. Perhaps we like it because it reminds us of ourselves, with its flat face, big eyes, cuddliness and playful ways. It sits up to eat, as we do. It has a simple black and white pattern and an easy name. It is rare and mysterious and very valuable. Sad to say, we have helped to make pandas even rarer and we will have to work hard to save them.

On the brighter side, the giant panda's urgent need for help has brought together conservation workers, vets, scientists, zoo-keepers and animal lovers from all over the world. The Chinese people and conservation organizations have managed to protect large areas of bamboo forest and guard the pandas that live in them. We have already found some ways of helping pandas to survive, by studying them in the wild and in captivity.

*Pandas can look very appealing. It is easy to see why they are so popular.*

If we can give enough support to the efforts to save pandas, perhaps in the next century there will be more pandas in the world than now. Then the panda on the WWF

*How long will pandas survive in the mountains of China?*

badge will be the symbol of a success story in wildlife conservation.

923350

# Glossary

**Artificial insemination**   A method people use to collect sperm from a male animal and put it into a female, while the two animals may be far apart.

**Breed**   To have babies.

**Breeding season**   The time of year when male and female animals come together to mate.

**Conservation**   Protection of animals and plants and the places they live in.

**Cub**   The word for a young panda.

**Digestion**   The way food is broken down inside the body.

**Expedition**   A long journey made by a team of people.

**Extinct**   Having died out. An animal is extinct when there are no more of its kind on earth.

**In captivity**   Kept in a zoo or animal collection.

**Mate**   To come together as a male and a female to have babies.

**Rare**   Very few in number.

**Reserve**   A wild place where plants and animals are protected in their natural surroundings.

**Solitary**   Living alone.

**Sperm**   A cell from a male animal, which joins with an egg from a female to start a baby.

**Starvation**   Having too little food to survive.

**Stud-book**   A list of the names and details of animals kept in captivity. It is used to plan breeding attempts in zoos.

**Unique**   Completely different from anything else.

**Vet**   The word "vet" is short for veterinary surgeon. An animal doctor.

**Zoology**   The scientific study of animals.

# Further reading

*Animals in the Wild: Panda* Mary Hoffman (Random, 1984)

*Book About Pandas* Ruth Gross (Scholastic, 1974)

*Endangered Animals* Malcolm Penny (Bookwright, 1988)

*Giant Pandas* O. Wong (Children's Press, 1987)

# Useful addresses

**Wildlife Preservation Trust International**
34th Street and Girard Ave.
Philadelphia, Pa. 19104

**Wildlife Rehabilitation Council**
P.O. Box 3007
Walnut Creek, Ca. 94598

**The Wildlife Society**
5410 Grosvenor Lane
Bethesda, Md. 20814

**World Wildlife Fund**
1601 Connecticut Ave., N.W.
Washington, D.C. 20009
(202) 293-4800

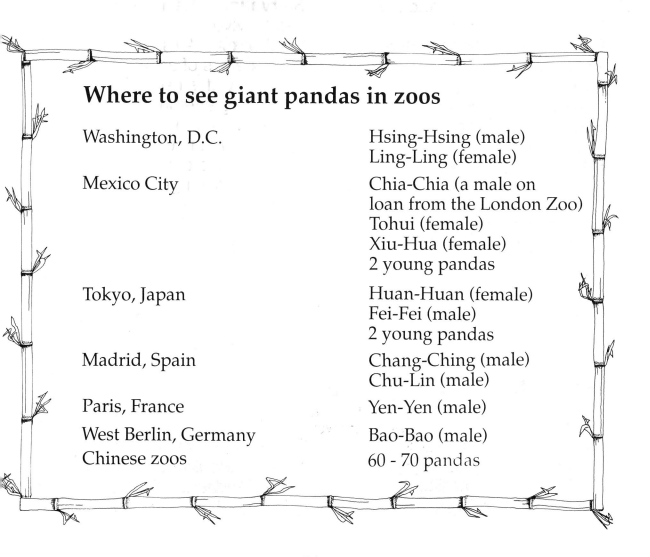

## Where to see giant pandas in zoos

| | |
|---|---|
| Washington, D.C. | Hsing-Hsing (male)<br>Ling-Ling (female) |
| Mexico City | Chia-Chia (a male on loan from the London Zoo)<br>Tohui (female)<br>Xiu-Hua (female)<br>2 young pandas |
| Tokyo, Japan | Huan-Huan (female)<br>Fei-Fei (male)<br>2 young pandas |
| Madrid, Spain | Chang-Ching (male)<br>Chu-Lin (male) |
| Paris, France | Yen-Yen (male) |
| West Berlin, Germany | Bao-Bao (male) |
| Chinese zoos | 60 - 70 pandas |

# Index

## Picture acknowledgments

The photographs in this book were reproduced by kind permission of the following: Bruce Coleman Ltd *cover* (John Cancalosi); 9 below (Gerald Cubitt); 14 (Freddy Mercay); 15 below, 27 (John MacKinnon); 23 (Norman Myers); 17 below, 20 above (WWF/Timm Rautert); 6 above (Hans Reinhard); 11, 13, 28 (WWF/Kojo Tanaka); 6 below, 9 above (Norman Tomalin). Okapia 16 (Christine Grzimek); 21, 22. Oxford Scientific Films 4, 29 (Zig Leszczynski); 12 (Animals Animals/Ralph Reinhold). Planet Earth Pictures 17 above (Franz Camenzind). Rex Features Ltd 18, 20 below, 24, 25. ZEFA 7, 19 (Dr. P. Thiele). Zoo Operations Ltd/John Knight 15 above. The artwork on pages 8, 11 and 31 is by Marilyn Clay.